Being Broke is Maddening

A Guide to Financial Wellness

By

A Renee' Johnson

Andrea Landry-Brown, CPRS

Being Broke is Maddening

© 2018 by A. Renee' Johnson & Andrea Landry-Brown, CPRS

All rights reserved. No part of this book may be reproduced, stored in a retrieval system or transmitted in any form or by any means without the prior written permission of the publishers, except by a reviewer who may quote brief passages in a review to be printed in a newspaper, magazine or journal.

First Printing

A²B Publishing
2303 Wheatley Dr. #104
Baltimore, MD 21207

www.asquaredbpublishing@gmail.com
www.andrealandrybrown.org
www.waotogether@gmail.com
www.anitarjohnson.com

A. Renee' Johnson

Andrea Landry-Brown, CPRS

Meet the Authors

Ms. Johnson is known as the Financial Behaviorist. She takes a holistic approach to money, focusing on enhancing your financial well-being, while understanding your emotional behavior around money. Once a client understands their anxiety around money, he/she can make clear and concise money decisions that will affect your legacy.

Ms. Landry-Brown, CPRS is known as the Mental Wellness Diva. She facilitates a variety of mental wellness programs that provide coping skills techniques, strengthens self-awareness, promotes self-advocacy, and welcomes hope in place of overwhelming confusion.

Being Broke is Maddening

Table of Contents

Section 1   Page 7

Financial Instability causes Mental Instability

Section 2   Page 18

Your Financial DNA-Where Does Those Financial Habits Come From?

Section 3   Page 30

From Financial Instability to Financial Stability Creating a Comfortable Mental Well-Being

Section 4   Page 44

Summary

A. Renee' Johnson

Andrea Landry-Brown, CPRS

Being Broke is Maddening

Introduction

Being able to understand your finances can be a complicated process that not only affects life's necessities but also your mental well-being. In this guide you will explore your financial DNA, how your money affects your mental health, turning your financial instability into financial stability leading to a better quality of life.

People have suffered from financial instability for years. You may have thought it was normal not sticking to a specific financial spending plan increasing your fear of money. These thoughts create a brainwashing belief that tracking your money is too time consuming therefore putting yourself deeper into debt. Not only are there simple ways to become **Financially Stable** but you can thrive to leave a legacy for your children.

Together, we will walk you through your **Financial Instability** to **Financial Wellness**. It will make a difference in your life.

A. Renee' Johnson

Andrea Landry-Brown, CPRS

Section 1
Financial Instability causes Mental Instability

Financial Instability

The Federal Reserve System (2008) explained financial instability as such: ***"When external events or market behaviors in the financial system are substantial enough to significantly distort or impair national or global financial markets, or to create significant risks for real aggregate economic performance."***

While this may be the best 'text book' definition the more appropriate 'personal' definition would characterize financial instability as: an inability to maintain a comfortable living for your family by living paycheck to paycheck, chronic unemployment

Being Broke is Maddening

or under-employment that doesn't pay a livable wage, a love-hate relationship with your money, failure to save money or balance your checkbook, the fear of creating (and sticking to) a financial spending plan, and the limited understanding of how personal DNA affects your decisions regarding your finances.

~ For a small piece of paper it carries a lot of weight! ~ (The O'Jays)

We are taught, at a very young age, that money makes the world go 'round. Money pays your bills, allows you to go on vacations, gives you the ability to purchase essential items (food, clothes, and miscellaneous items), and buys houses and cars. Let's face it… we need money for *everything*!

~ People facing wide monthly swings in income and expenses need more than better budgeting skills or financial literacy education. ~ (Ogden & Morduch, 2017)

Living Paycheck to Paycheck

You may be conditioned to finding the kind of job that will supply you with just

A. Renee' Johnson

Andrea Landry-Brown, CPRS

enough money that satisfies the demands of life. This kind of employment accommodations keep you on the brink of being broke because you haven't negotiated the type of salary that will supply the money needed for life's necessities and a little bit extra. As a result, you balance your money (to the best of your ability) with your responsibilities of home, family, and life. Living paycheck to paycheck means you have paved a specific route for your money to travel and sustain a wavering tightrope for you to walk until your next paycheck gets deposited.

Chronic Unemployment
Under-Employment

There are many reasons for chronic unemployment (too many for us to list within this book) but the overall consensus of chronic unemployment is the same; and that is lack of an income. If you are laid off or fired for unjust causes, then you could qualify for unemployment insurance. While unemployment insurance provides you with some financial help it does not guarantee a sustainable living wage. Unemployment insurance is temporary and usually gives you a quarter of what your regular

Being Broke is Maddening

earnings were which puts you in an unstable financial predicament.

Ultimately, you will choose employment to earn an income that sustains your life. Unfortunately, the job you chose may not utilize your full employment potential (under-employment). Under-Employment is often frustrating because you know you could be working in a company that will increase your talents and help you promote with the potential of making more money and receiving lucrative benefits. Both unemployment and under-employment contribute to financial instability, simply because they are unpredictable. While unemployment insurance has a discontinuation date, under-employment could result in you quitting because you are overqualified and have found better employment opportunities.

Love / Hate Relationship

People love to earn and spend money. Think of how much fun you have when you're out shopping. You're buying that pair of jeans you found on sale, those sneakers you need for basketball, the watch your mother always wanted, or the car you needed for work. The freedom that comes with having the money to get the things you want is invigorating. In contrast, you hate the bills that come in the mail every month (gas & electric, water & trash, car / house / life insurance, rent, cable & internet and credit card). Now you have to share your money with the necessities of life. Sometimes you take money from those bills to treat yourself to something you like. After all... you *earned* it! Then you chastise yourself for being reckless and not taking care of business.

Failure to Save Money

How often do you tell yourself, "I need to save some money!"? This is usually an after thought when you've mapped out all the things you *need* to spend money on. Truth be told, when you have a lack of funds to take care of your basic needs the last thing on your mind is *saving* money. Unfortunately, when you don't make saving money a priority (along with paying bills) then you short change yourself into constantly being broke causing madness (just like the title of this book!). Failure to save leads to financial instability because you have failed to provide yourself with a cushion for life's unpredictable upsets or delights.

Being Broke is Maddening

Financial Spending Plan

Now comes the dreaded part of this book… your financial spending plan. Most people believe a financial spending plan consists of the essential things (bills, food, transportation and clothing) and a few Miscellaneous things (grooming, gym memberships, or credit cards). We rarely consider the nonchalant things we spend money on, such as: lunch, coffee, snacks and retail therapy. Over time these small expenses add up. When you don't create a specific financial spending plan that details all the things you spend money on, ***and*** stick to it, then you sink into financial instability.

Mental Instability

Mental instability is likened unto mental illness. <u>***I must be clear***</u>… to be mentally unstable does ***not*** mean you have a mental illness. However, in some cases, mental instability could lead to mental illness and often has the same symptoms as mental illness. According to the Merriam-Webster Dictionary.com (2018) mental means: ***"of or relating to the mind, specifically relating to the total emotional and intellectual response of an***

A. Renee' Johnson

Andrea Landry-Brown, CPRS

individual to external reality." **Instability means:** *"The quality or state of being unstable."*

For the purposes of this book we're going to identify *mental instability* as strong emotional reactions to unstable thinking.

Financial Instability causing Mental Instability

Your mental health will be adversely affected when you do not take the time to intelligently create an adequate financial plan so your money will work for **_you_** while you are working for your **_money_**.

How many times have you told yourself, "I have more month than money" because you did not manage your finances in a way to have money to carry you through the end of the month? When you don't have the money you need, your frustration runs rampant creating exhaustion and mental instability causing isolation, shame, avoidance, anxiety and depression.

Being Broke is Maddening

Isolation

There are many things you can engage in that do not require money; but most activities cost a nominal fee. If you do not have the money to pay your way through whatever adventures you participate in, then you may make excuses to get out of doing what you enjoy doing. This self-imposed isolation prevents embarrassment around others, because you don't want to confess the fact you're broke.

Shame

You work hard, everyday, and still don't have the money you need to pay every bill, buy enough food, put gas in your vehicle each week or pay for transportation (Lyft, Uber, taxi, or public transportation), or even have lunch with your co-workers. Being broke creates a deep shaming cycle that is demeaning and crushing to your self-esteem as you begin to berate yourself for not having enough money to take care of your necessities due to:
- o The day you missed work because you were ill.
- o You needed a mental health day.

A. Renee' Johnson

Andrea Landry-Brown, CPRS

- You didn't get getting the promotion you needed to give you more income.
- You didn't save aside money.

Avoidance

When your debt is more than the amount you make and you have participated in the 'robbing Peter to pay Paul' practice until you are unable to do that any longer, then you play the 'avoidance' game with your debt. What this means is: you pretend you didn't see the bills when they come, or you pick and choose which ones have priority and pay them while leaving the others behind. This tactic only builds your debt and your telephone rings off the hook because the collectors are threatening you with liens to get the money owed for their accounts. According to Brad Klontz, in a 2010 article for Psychology Today, 'money avoidance' can be described as a 'disorder'. Klontz states, that people will go into denial **"rather than face financial reality. People try to minimize money problems by refusing to think about them all together."** (2010)

Being Broke is Maddening

Anxiety

Anxiety is a mood disorder that can cause you to hyperventilate, feel tightness in your chest, extremely nervous, irritable, create paranoia, and have racing thoughts. When you don't have enough money to take care of your needs all of these feelings can overcome you and feel overwhelming. You may find yourself borrowing money, taking money from other avenues to take care of immediate needs, or selling valuable belongings to get money.

Depression

This mood disorder causes you to lose motivation and have the feeling of wanting to give up because nothing you try will ever pan out. You have worked your usual 40 hour week, and even put in some overtime. After paying taxes you have very little money over what your regular paycheck is. This can be very disconcerting, weighing heavily on your mind about what to do next. You've tried everything you could think of to generate an income, shelled out the money needed for your essentials and not you have nothing to show for it. Depression may become a familiar friend.

A. Renee' Johnson

Andrea Landry-Brown, CPRS

You will find yourself putting off important tasks and bills, and in some cases giving up the desire to try.

    This chapter is focused on helping you understand how financial instability could create mental instability. As we move further along this journey, we are going to dive deeper into your financial DNA and why you harbor the relationship with your money you have. We've taken a glance at how easy it is to slip into financial instability and how that affects your mental health. Our intention is to provide tools and guidelines for you to become financially stable, strengthening your mental well-being. So, hang on tight… it's gonna be a bumpy ride but well worth it!

Being Broke is Maddening

Section 2

Your Financial DNA
Where Does Those Financial Habits Come From?

When your parents conceived you, they combined every aspect of their being into the person you were going to become for the rest of your life. Your DNA provides the roadmap for your eye and hair color, how short or tall you will be, your personality, and your decision-making processes. This also includes your relationship with money! Did you know you had a relationship with money since before you ever laid eyes (or hands) on it? In this segment, we're gonna get all up in your business to demonstrate to you how you developed your association with your finances. The factors that play a major role in how you relate to money are: the genesis of your financial relationship; your finances and religious obligations; understanding the importance of your financial

A. Renee' Johnson

Andrea Landry-Brown, CPRS

relationship; lastly, achieving money successes through self-efficacy

The Genesis of Your Financial Relationship.

Have you ever wondered how your financial habits were developed? Well, think back to the people you had your very first contact with. Normally your learned behaviors come from family, friends, loved ones and guardians. The same is to be said when it comes to your finances. Your financial relationship was established by watching how the people in your life handled money. The hierarchy (one or two parent home) within your household influences your financial future. In a two-parent home there are three monetary conversations that could take place.

1) The parents practice the rule of marriage where everything is an equal decision-making process as to how the finances are distributed.
2) The parent that makes the most money dominates the household (this could cause stress and mistrust).

Being Broke is Maddening

3) Both parents recognize their strengths and weaknesses and have agreed that a specific parent will take care of the financial issues, while the other parent takes care of everything else.

In a one parent home there is only one person who has control over every aspect of the finances. What makes financial decisions interesting, in this scenario, is how well the single parent can manage the needs of the family, personal needs and the need to pay debtors.

Think back to your childhood…

What was your first contact with money?

_____

_____

_____

Did you have an allowance? If you did, how much and if not, why not?

_____

_____

A. Renee' Johnson

Andrea Landry-Brown, CPRS

Did you grow up in a one or two parent household?   1 / 2

If you grew up in a two-parent home, what kind of uncomfortable conversations about money did your parents have? _____

_____

_____

Did your parents plan life around their finances or were they very spontaneous? _____

_____

Did you witness your parents fighting about not having enough money for basic needs or special family events?   Yes / No

What financial agreements did your parents have? _____

_____

_____

Being Broke is Maddening

Which parent was in charge of financial decision making? _____

How did this make you feel? _____

_____

_____

If you were raised in a one parent home, how did your parent / guardian manage money?

_____

_____

Did your parent / guardian borrow money from someone else? If so, who and if not, what did he / she do for money when there wasn't enough?

_____

_____

_____

Experiencing your parent's negative relationship with money can make you fearful of discussing finances with your future partner or make you feel inferior because you earn less than your partner. Living with your parent's

A. Renee' Johnson

Andrea Landry-Brown, CPRS

patterns could create a money script that reads of, "I am not worthy of having the best." or "I am entitled to everything I want (without consequence)." These motivations / habits could cause you to overspend to compensate for your feelings.

Take a moment to think about which family member you inherited your financial behaviors from:

- Mother
- Father
- Step-Parent
- Guardian
- Siblings
- Grandparents
- Cousins
- Friends
- Loved Ones

What did you learn from any of these individuals? _____

_____

_____

Being Broke is Maddening

Your Finances and Religious Obligations

Most religions, no matter your affiliation, has a financial requirement (tithe / offerings / sacrifice). Usually the requested amount is 10% of your total earnings. This act of commitment helps you honor your faith in whatever religion you practice. The act of tithing / offering / sacrifice is to guarantee your faith in the multitudes of blessings you were promised to receive. Your faith, and belief in God / Allah / Buddha / Jehovah (insert deity here _____) dictates your financial responsibility to your place of worship and how the blessings are returned to you.

What religious belief do you choose to follow?
_____

_____

What is your financial responsibility to your religious organization? _____

_____

How does your tithes / offerings / sacrifice fit into your finances? _____

_____

Do you feel guilty if you do not pay your tithes / offerings / sacrifice?   Yes / No

How does your tithes / offerings / sacrifice benefit you? _____

_____

Now that you have a general idea of where your thoughts of money come from the understanding of your **Financial Relationship** is becoming clearer.

Understanding the Importance of Your Financial Relationship

Step one in the process of having healthy financial habits is to know where your behavior towards money comes from. Your Financial DNA plays an important part in understanding why you do what you do with your money. Earlier we explored your parents / caregiver's relationship with money which encouraged your connection with money. You gained an explanation as to why you either overspend or are frugal with your finances. You may consider clothes more important than food. Could it be

Being Broke is Maddening

your parents / caregivers thought more about your appearance than putting food on the table?

You can create healthier financial habits that include tracking you're spending, creating a reasonable Financial Spending Plan (**FSP**) and even an achievable investment plan. These practices will aid you in improving the following:

- o Your mental and physical health.
- o Your social life.
- o Your problem-solving skills.
- o Your living conditions.

What are some other areas of your life that will have a significant improvement when you adopt healthier spending practices?

_____

_____

Achieving Money Successes through Self-Efficacy

Self-efficacy is a person's belief in his or her ability to succeed in during challenging situations (Cherry, 2018).

A. Renee' Johnson

Andrea Landry-Brown, CPRS

You might think that self-efficacy sounds like to self-esteem or self-confidence; but they don't quite hit the mark. Self-efficacy is more the act of achieving success through "doing." Actively participating in the actions that aid you in having a successful relationship with your finances. This includes implementing better behaviors that make a way for better decisions. Tracking each dollar you spend without making excuses as to *why* you spent that money, will help you understand where your money is going. Creating an effective tracking system (with a variety of personalized categories) will aid you in incorporating your money into your **FSP**. Your **FSP** is more beneficial to you than a *budget* because it goes beyond just calculating your month to month projected spending patterns; which in a sense causes you to spend your money like it's on a diet. The **Financial Spending Plan** allows you to calculate your *actual spending* over a three month period; as opposed to your monthly *projected spending*, to get a more accurate accounting of your finances.

Let's go a step further… we are encouraging you to create financial affirmations

Being Broke is Maddening

along with your **FSP** (which we will create in Section 3). I know, you're thinking "What are they talking about, financial affirmations?!" When you are trying to improve your mental health you utilize positive affirmations in the form of "I am worthy of love and will love me through all my faults." Well, the same idea applies. Use your powers of positive visualization and see yourself living comfortably with the money you need to take care of your essential needs, pay off your debts, save for a rainy day, or treat your family to a fun vacation. Say a positive affirmation like "Money comes to me easily and effortlessly, through various income streams." You may also want to consider creating a **Financial Action Board**. A financial action board is different than a vision board in that you will utilize visual guides that associate with the methods in which you would like to receive financial stability. When creating your financial action board, keep in mind your personal dreams about money with a clear method of how to make those goals a reality.

A. Renee' Johnson

Andrea Landry-Brown, CPRS

What are some other methods you could participate in to help you reach your financial success? _____

_____

Give yourself an exact date to accomplish this goal. What is your goal date? _____

Being Broke is Maddening

Section 3

From Financial Instability to Financial Stability Creating a Comfortable Mental Well-Being

~ When you have financial stability, you don't

---

have to stress about money and you can focus your energy on other parts of your life. ~
(Silva, 2018)

In section one we talked about what financial instability looks like and how it affects your mental well-being. We're going to dive into what financial stability is and how to achieve it while welcoming mental wellness.

Financial Stability

The definition for financial stability is deeply personal and has a different meaning for

A. Renee' Johnson

Andrea Landry-Brown, CPRS

everyone. For the purpose of this book we will define **financial stability** as such: ***the ability to pay for all of life's necessities with money left over for savings for life's uncertainties creating personal monetary freedom.***

A universal view of financial stability is the ability to have enough money to pay for your bills, set aside money for future goals and have funds for emergency circumstances. While the ultimate method of achieving financial stability is to create an effective financial spending plan (**FSP**), there are other methods of accomplishing your money goals. You can achieve your financial freedom by (Silva, 2018):

- o Investing in yourself
- o Clearing your debts
- o Having a 'rainy day' fund
- o Remembering to have fun

Investing in Yourself

This is probably the most unique topic of the entire book, however, when you think about

Being Broke is Maddening

how to improve *you* then you can increase your net worth in life and in employment possibilities. If you need to get your General Education Degree (GED) then make the effort to study and obtain that degree. It may seem like a small thing, but it really does make a difference in your life and your employable skill level. This not only shows employers that you thought enough of yourself to complete your high school education, but that you kept a valuable commitment to yourself. This means you are capable of being loyal to an employer as well. Improve your customer service and office skills by taking technical courses or investing in webinars that guide you in the best tactics which make you a more desirable candidate for your ideal employment choice.

Clearing Your Debts

Paying off your debts may be the most difficult task to complete; however, it is achievable. Many credit card companies encourage their customers to pay about $20

more than their minimum payment due to help them raise their credit score and pay off their balance quicker.

A. Renee' Johnson

Andrea Landry-Brown, CPRS

Some utility companies try to assist their customers with their bills by offering the ability to pay the average balance of their monthly bill. What this option does is offer the possibility to have some extra money saved with the company for the moments when your utility usage fluctuates (during the summer and winter months) causing a larger bill at the end of the year because the company kept your bill the same during the months when fluctuation happens.

While your cable, water & trash, cellular telephone and transportation costs don't offer the opportunity to have the same cost each month, you can still pay a little extra on each bill (with the exception of your transportation cost) to build up a little equity to make the next month's bill more cost effective and affording you the ability to save a little money aside.

Rainy Day Fund

Remember when your grandparents told you to save for a 'rainy day'? They were referring to emergency situations and times when you wanted to treat yourself to a 'big ticket' item (i.e. car, vacation, expensive

Being Broke is Maddening

jewelry or clothing). Your bank offers a savings account and a 'Christmas' (a special savings account for shopping) account. Taking a moment to save aside just a little bit per check (for example: an extra $5 or $10) can add up over time. Treat these savings accounts like you would your retirement plans, like they don't exist! If you allow the bank to take a certain amount from your direct deposit, every check, and put it into a special savings account you can have money put away for special moments or when life throws you an unexpected curve ball.

Remember to Have Fun!

Of all the choices Mr. Silva provided in his Smart Asset article (2018), having fun is the most delightful. He mentions how people get so caught up in trying to take care of business that fun is the furthest from consideration. However, the old adage of all work and no play can be stressful is very true! You must allow yourself some fun. There are many fun things you can do that are inexpensive, and sometimes free. You can still schedule a special treat for yourself, and your family, once in a while. Maybe once a

month you could plan a family roller skating night, trip to the zoo, or dinner. You can also

A. Renee' Johnson

Andrea Landry-Brown, CPRS

have family fun night at home with games (board, card and video), or take a drive to the park or beach.

Creating an Effective Financial Spending Plan (FSP)

The most important method of creating financial stability is creating an effective financial spending plan. Without a spending plan nothing you do is going to matter because you are not actively tracking your spending behaviors or your money (incoming or outgoing).

Your FSP is like creating a budget but it's a more efficient method. A budget limits you to proposing what you **_could_** spend on life's necessities. Therefor we state a budget could be seen as **_money on a diet_**, because just like a diet it is unpredictable. So, we encourage

you to never budgetize your money again, instead use your spending plan for more stability in your finances. An FSP gives you more flexibility because you track the **_actual_** amounts you spend on life's necessities during a

Being Broke is Maddening

three-month period. Just like a job gives you a 90-day probationary period, you give your money a 90-day evaluation to effectively create a plan to give you more financial freedom.

We've given you an initial FSP grid to begin considering what you're spending your money on. There are three extra grids in the book for you to continue your planning. We encourage you to update your grids as needed to always have a method of financial stability.

Fill Out the Financial Spending Grid (FSP)

Rent		*Cable / Internet*	
Gas & Electric		*Cellular Telephone*	
Water & Trash		*Gas / Public Transportation / Uber – Lyft - Taxi*	
Food		*Laundry / Dry Cleaning*	
Car Payment		*Clothing*	
Car Insurance		*Credit Card*	

A. Renee' Johnson

Andrea Landry-Brown, CPRS

Health & Life Insurance		*Savings*	
	TOTAL AMOUNT		

How much do you spend on your Miscellaneous items?

Food / Lunch		Coffee	
Paper & Pens		Snacks	
Jewelry		Hats	
Home Care (dishes & decorative items)		Grooming Products	
Movies		Perfume /	

Being Broke is Maddening

(DVD & Theater)		Cologne	
Car Care		Electronic Items	
Pay Per View		Gifts	

List other Miscellaneous items, and how much you spend on them, here: _____

_____

_____

Next, calculate the amount of the extra Miscellaneous items along with your financial spending plan amount: _____

Add an additional 5% to 10% to the amount you have calculated to allow for unexpected family challenges (pregnancy, illness, death), holidays, birthdays and / or emergencies.

A. Renee' Johnson

Andrea Landry-Brown, CPRS

Your Income

Your Money Coming In	
Employment Income	
SSI / SSDI Income	
State Disability Income	
Unemployment Insurance	
Child / Spousal Support	
Business Income	
Your Side Hustle Income	
Total	

Being Broke is Maddening

Miscellaneous Income	
Lottery	
Personal Items for Sale	
Monetary Gifts	
Other Income	
Total	
Combined Total	

Keep in mind, Miscellaneous income is not stable income and can include several things you consider incoming financial support.

Let's do the math and make the magic happen.

Your Income Amount: _____
Amount from FSP: _____

Amount from Misc. Income: _____

A. Renee' Johnson

Andrea Landry-Brown, CPRS

Please subtract your FSB from your Income Amount:

_____ - _____ = _____
FSP   **Income**   **Your Money**

Several things we want you to take notice of:

- ➤ Your income fluctuates from month to month, unless you have a salaried position that pays you a set amount.
- ➤ Your Miscellaneous income is not always a reliable source of finances. Therefore, we did not calculate that money in the above scenario.
- ➤ The amount of some of your bills also fluctuate from month to month.

Remembering these points will alleviate some of the stress behind your plan and help you figure the money you can save aside for the future or your 'rainy day'.

These planning methods are a great tool to help you identify your spending habits and identify problem areas where you spend money (unconsciously) without considering the long-term effects of the money you will need later.

Being Broke is Maddening

Take some time to ask yourself if you really need some of the things on your **FSP** or **Misc. Items** list. Consider letting go some of your debt (Do you need more than one cell phone line? Do you watch 200 channels on television? Do you need the triple play cable package? Etc.). It may behoove you to consult a debt consolidation counselor to create one bill for your outstanding debts or to reach out to creditors that can expel your debt that is no longer viable. You could also tackle one debt at a time. Some of the debt collectors have the option to pay a small lump sum (that could be half of what you owe) and the debt is forgiven. Or, you could make a plan to make payment arrangements where an agreed upon amount is paid each month for a specific amount of time (example: paying $150 every two weeks for 8 months). Companies would rather you pay *something* than nothing at all, and it looks good on your credit report.

A. Renee' Johnson

Andrea Landry-Brown, CPRS

Financial Stability = Mental Well-Being

You have gone through the process to be financially stable… how does it feel?

_____
_____
_____

Your mental health consists of your emotions, thought processes and overall feelings. In the first section we discussed how lack of money caused isolation, shame, avoidance, anxiety and depression. When you have a successful plan in place, and you are actively participating in that strategy, your outlook on life changes. Your stress level decreases causing a reduction in anxiety. You may make commitments with family, friends, co-workers and associates to participate in luncheons or other outings (still being mindful of your spending plan, you don't want to go backwards falling into the same trap). Your self-esteem grows stronger building your excitement for things you love to enjoy now that you're not losing sleep over how to take care of yourself and your family. When you are financially stable your confidence shines.

Being Broke is Maddening

Section 4

Summary

Within these pages we have dived into the complex and intimate relationship you have had with money since your conception. You have taken the time to explore how you think about your finances and how your spending patterns affect your quality of life.

We have offered you tools to eliminate some of your negative thought patterns, while providing you with an FSP to encourage you to be mindful every time you take out your debit / credit card to pay for anything. When you're on a diet to help maintain your weight you may feel the need to indulge (on occasion) to a special treat. This treat may not immediately affect your diet plans, but in the long run it could reverse the weight you had planned to lose. The same concept applies to your plan for your money. If you splurge on that special treat to reward you for your ability

A. Renee' Johnson

Andrea Landry-Brown, CPRS

to save, it may not have an immediate affect on your finances. However, it may take away from a debt you were trying to pay off or a bill that is due.

Make copies of the FSP grid and keep one in your wallet / purse (especially the Miscellaneous grid) so that you can keep track of the money you spend as you spend it.

We hope these tools will benefit you and positively grow your money bringing you financial mental wellness stability.

Being Broke is Maddening

Extra FSP Grid's

Fill Out the Financial Spending Grid (FSP)

Rent		*Cable / Internet*	
Gas & Electric		*Cellular Telephone*	
Water & Trash		*Gas / Public Transportation / Uber – Lyft - Taxi*	
Food		*Laundry / Dry Cleaning*	
Car Payment		*Clothing*	
Car Insurance		*Credit Card*	
Health & Life Insurance		*Savings*	
TOTAL AMOUNT			

A. Renee' Johnson

Andrea Landry-Brown, CPRS

How much do you spend on your Miscellaneous items?

Food / Lunch		Coffee	
Paper & Pens		Snacks	
Jewelry		Hats	
Home Care (dishes & decorative items)		Grooming Products	
Movies (DVD & Theater)		Perfume / Cologne	
Car Care		Electronic Items	
Pay Per View		Gifts	

Being Broke is Maddening

List other Miscellaneous items, and how much you spend on them, here: _____
_____
_____
_____

Next, calculate the amount of the extra Miscellaneous items along with your financial spending plan amount: _____

Add an additional 5% to 10% to the amount you have calculated to allow for unexpected family challenges (pregnancy, illness, death), holidays, birthdays and / or emergencies.

Your Income

Your Money Coming In	
Employment Income	
SSI / SSDI Income	
State Disability Income	

A. Renee' Johnson

Unemployment Insurance	
Child / Spousal Support	
Business Income	
Your Side Hustle Income	
Total	
Miscellaneous Income	
Lottery	
Personal Items for Sale	
Monetary Gifts	
Other Income	
Total	

Being Broke is Maddening

Combined Total	

Keep in mind, Miscellaneous income is not stable income and can include a number of things you consider incoming financial support.

Let's do the math and make the magic happen.

Your Income Amount: _____
Amount from FSP: _____
Amount from Misc. Income: _____

Please subtract your FSB from your Income Amount:

_____ - _____ = _____
   FSP   **Income**   **Your Money**

A. Renee' Johnson

Andrea Landry-Brown, CPRS

Fill Out the Financial Spending Grid (FSP)

Rent		Cable / Internet	
Gas & Electric		Cellular Telephone	
Water & Trash		Gas / Public Transportation / Uber – Lyft - Taxi	
Food		Laundry / Dry Cleaning	
Car Payment		Clothing	
Car Insurance		Credit Card	
Health & Life Insurance		Savings	
TOTAL AMOUNT			

Being Broke is Maddening

How much do you spend on your Miscellaneous items?

Food / Lunch		**Coffee**	
Paper & Pens		**Snacks**	
Jewelry		**Hats**	
Home Care (dishes & decorative items)		**Grooming Products**	
Movies (DVD & Theater)		**Perfume / Cologne**	
Car Care		**Electronic Items**	
Pay Per View		**Gifts**	

A. Renee' Johnson

Andrea Landry-Brown, CPRS

List other Miscellaneous items, and how much you spend on them, here: _____

_____

_____

_____

Next, calculate the amount of the extra Miscellaneous items along with your financial spending plan amount: _____

Add an additional 5% to 10% to the amount you have calculated to allow for unexpected family challenges (pregnancy, illness, death), holidays, birthdays and / or emergencies.

Your Income

Your Money Coming In	
Employment Income	
SSI / SSDI Income	

Being Broke is Maddening

State Disability Income	
Unemployment Insurance	
Child / Spousal Support	
Business Income	
Your Side Hustle Income	
Total	
Miscellaneous Income	
Lottery	
Personal Items for Sale	
Monetary Gifts	
Other Income	

A. Renee' Johnson

Andrea Landry-Brown, CPRS

	Total	
	Combined Total	

Keep in mind, Miscellaneous income is not stable income and can include a number of things you consider incoming financial support.

Let's do the math and make the magic happen.

Your Income Amount: _____
Amount from FSP: _____
Amount from Misc. Income: _____

Please subtract your FSB from your Income Amount:

_____ - _____ = _____
  FSP   **Income**   **Your Money**

Being Broke is Maddening

Fill Out the Financial Spending Grid (FSP)

Rent		Cable / Internet	
Gas & Electric		Cellular Telephone	
Water & Trash		Gas / Public Transportation / Uber – Lyft - Taxi	
Food		Laundry / Dry Cleaning	
Car Payment		Clothing	
Car Insurance		Credit Card	
Health & Life Insurance		Savings	
TOTAL AMOUNT			

A. Renee' Johnson

Andrea Landry-Brown, CPRS

How much do you spend on your Miscellaneous items?

Food / Lunch		Coffee	
Paper & Pens		Snacks	
Jewelry		Hats	
Home Care (dishes & decorative items)		Grooming Products	
Movies (DVD & Theater)		Perfume / Cologne	
Car Care		Electronic Items	
Pay Per View		Gifts	

Being Broke is Maddening

List other Miscellaneous items, and how much you spend on them, here: _____
_____
_____

Next, calculate the amount of the extra Miscellaneous items along with your financial spending plan amount: _____

Add an additional 5% to 10% to the amount you have calculated to allow for unexpected family challenges (pregnancy, illness, death), holidays, birthdays and / or emergencies.

Your Income

Your Money Coming In	
Employment Income	
SSI / SSDI Income	
State Disability Income	

A. Renee' Johnson

Andrea Landry-Brown, CPRS

Unemployment Insurance	
Child / Spousal Support	
Business Income	
Your Side Hustle Income	
Total	
Miscellaneous Income	
Lottery	
Personal Items for Sale	
Monetary Gifts	
Other Income	
Total	

Being Broke is Maddening

Combined Total	

Keep in mind, Miscellaneous income is not stable income and can include a number of things you consider incoming financial support.

Let's do the math and make the magic happen.

Your Income Amount: _____
Amount from FSP: _____
Amount from Misc. Income: _____

Please subtract your FSB from your Income Amount:

_____ - _____ = _____
FSP   **Income**   **Your Money**

A. Renee' Johnson

Andrea Landry-Brown, CPRS

Resources

Cherry, K. (2018). Self-Efficacy: Why Believing in Yourself Matters. Retrieved from https://www.verywellmind.com/what-is-self-efficacy-2795954
Financial Instability (2018). Retrieved from https://definedterm.com/financial_instability

Instability (2018). Retrieved from https://www.merriam-webster.com/dictionary/instability

Klontz, Psy.D., CFP, B. (2010). Do You Have a Money Disorder?. Retrieved from https://www.psychologytoday.com/us/blog/mind-over-money/201001/do-you-have-money-disorder

Ogden, T., Murdock, J. (2017). Too Many Americans Suffer from Financial Instability. Their Employers Can Help Fix It. Retrieved from https://hbr.org/2017/12/too-many-americans-suffer-from-financial-instability-their-employers-can-help-fix-it

Silva, CEPF, D. (2018). 10 Steps to Reach Financial Stability. Retrieved from https://smartasset.com/retirement/10-steps-to-reach-financial-stability

www.ingramcontent.com/pod-product-compliance
Lightning Source LLC
Chambersburg PA
CBHW071433220526
45469CB00004B/1513